DREAMSCAPE ORACLE

978 6467 0553

By Matt Hughes

Copyright © 2021 U.S. Games Systems, Inc.

All rights reserved. The illustrations, cover design, and contents are protected by copyright. No part of this booklet may be reproduced in any form without permission in writing from the publisher, except by a reviewer who wishes to quote brief passages in connection with a review written for inclusion in a magazine, newspaper or website.

First Edition

10 9 8 7 6 5 4

Made in China

Published by
U.S. GAMES SYSTEMS, INC.
179 Ludlow Street
Stamford, CT 06902 USA
www.usgamesinc.com

Thank you to Sarah Swisher for being such a big supporter of this project and helping us bring it to life.

A very special thank you to Jaymi Elford for her amazing talent of writing and storytelling.

~

*"A person is the product of their dreams.
So make sure to dream great dreams.
And then try to live
your dream."*

~ Maya Angelou

CONTENTS

Introduction 7

The Dreamscape Card Meanings 8

The Architect 11

The Spring 13

The Night 15

The Light 17

The Gate 19

The Prophet 21

The Serpent 23

Death Mother 25

Memory 27

Rabbit and Fox 29

The Shadow 31

The Seer 33

The Scales 35

The Path 37

Balance 39

The Gift 41

Luna Moth 43

The Silence	45
The Word	47
White Buffalo	49
The Selkie	51
Raven	53
Koi Fish	55
Elephant	57
White Owl	59
Octopus	61
Sun Bear	63
Harpy Eagle	65
Fawn	67
Tiger	69
Palomino	71
Sea Turtle	73
The Dreamscape Oracle Spread	74
Performing Your First Reading	75
About the Artist	77

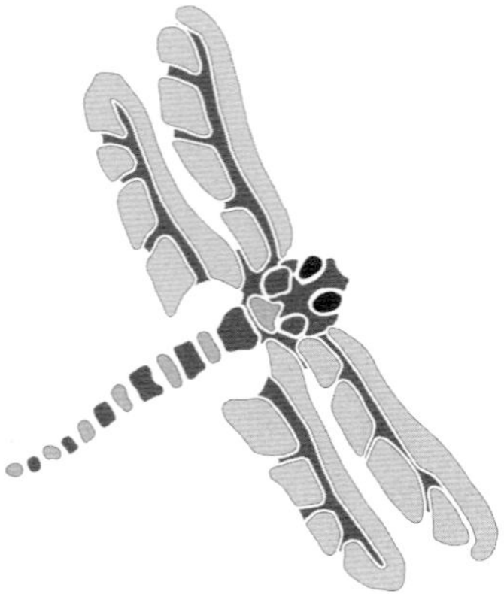

INTRODUCTION

Dreams are natural portals into another realm of consciousness where we see the unseen and comprehend the incomprehensible. We are not alone in this other world; we have guides that help us understand visions unveiled during dreamtime. These guides appear on each card of the *Dreamscape Oracle*. They can be used to help you understand the messages your higher self or external voices send out. Let this *Dreamscape Oracle* guidebook assist you in interpreting the messages you receive.

The *Dreamscape Oracle* is a cartomancy deck that consists of 32 cards. In addition to being a stand-alone divination deck, it is also a companion to the *Ethereal Visions Tarot*. Many of the figures appearing in the imagery are based on mythological archetypes from all over the world. These archetypes come together to help us explore the liminal spaces in our lives.

The dragonfly is a winged messenger that flies between worlds. We chose it to appear on the card back because it is a perfect companion to guide you into using this deck. This beautiful creature zips through the realms guided by the voice and light of the moon. Dragonfly whispers messages into our ears as we sleep. These messages from our guides manifest as dreams for us to interact with and respond to. The ever-vigilant messenger delivers our questions, fears, and responses back through to the other world for those who dwell betwixt and between to create new dreams for us to experience.

Let the imagery in this deck whisper stories into your mind. Feel the archetypes' power as they draw you into the dream world and reveal what's deep within, beyond the portals.

THE DREAMSCAPE CARD MEANINGS

This booklet contains information for each of the 32 cards. We have taken care and intention to honor the culture for every archetype represented on this deck. Many stories come from mythology or fairy tales that inspired us in our childhood. Each description gives some background into the culture it came from and guidance on how you can use this information to gain insight into your life and the questions you have.

The information in this booklet is just a starting point. Trust your intuition as you gaze into the cards. It will give you a lot more insight, suggesting new ways the deck can influence the questions you ask it. Assigning meaning to your question may not come easily. It takes time and practice to decipher what the cards say, especially when many cards appear. Slow down and give your intuition space to communicate with the cards.

Close your eyes and open your mind to the world of possibilities each card reveals to you. Take a deep breath and allow the image on each card to connect with your intuition. If the message within your body conflicts with what the card imagery tells you, go with what your body tells you. Performing a divination reading blends the art of storytelling with the symbolism embedded in each card. Understanding the lexicon takes practice. Enjoy this process. There are no wrong answers in interpreting the cards.

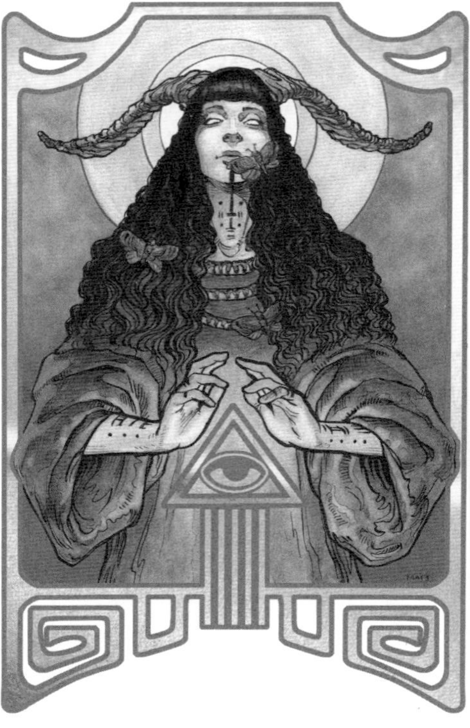

THE ARCHITECT

The Architect is a mysterious figure. Their eyes appear wide open, yet blurred by the state of flow. They honor the creative state, which holds the key to unlock the plan made inside their mind. When the Architect begins a new idea, they close their eyes and give into the creation within. When they have the item fully formed in their mind's eye, they can work their magic to make it a reality. The horns on their head direct the power required to make magic happen. Their hands are relaxed, releasing the energy of the Architect's design. The Masonic Eye appears within the space between their hands. This symbol reminds the Architect of their ability to manifest their divine will. A butterfly hovers near the Architect's tattooed face, bringing new creations and designs to their capabilities.

Meanings: Create your own life; use your mental powers to manifest desires.

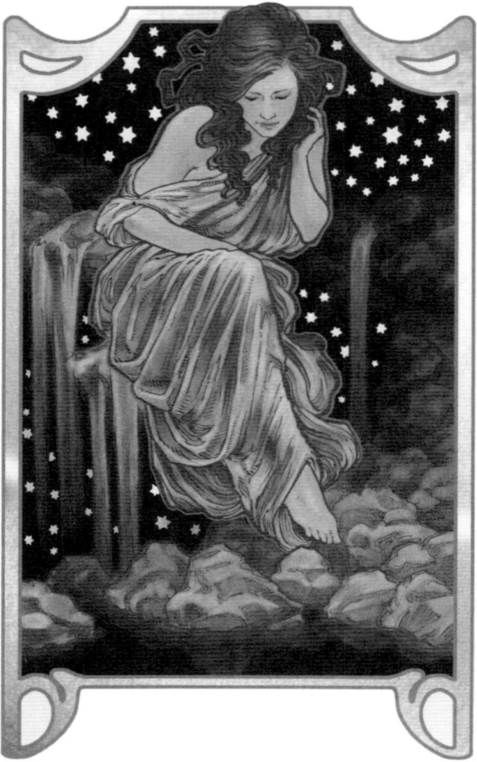

THE SPRING

A red-headed maiden sits at the edge of the sacred waters. She leans forward, seeking out images and answers from the surface of the pool. She has a desire to belong, to fit in with her kin. Stars stretch across the sky behind her, illuminating the blackness. The light enables her to see clearly and to follow the path. Each star is a gift of hope, a promise that a better future will come, no matter what. Many waterfalls and springs flow around the Maiden. Water is a healing symbol, as the springs bring life-sustaining nutrients to every living creature, both sick and healthy.

Meanings: Allow water to cure you; release your emotions and anxieties.

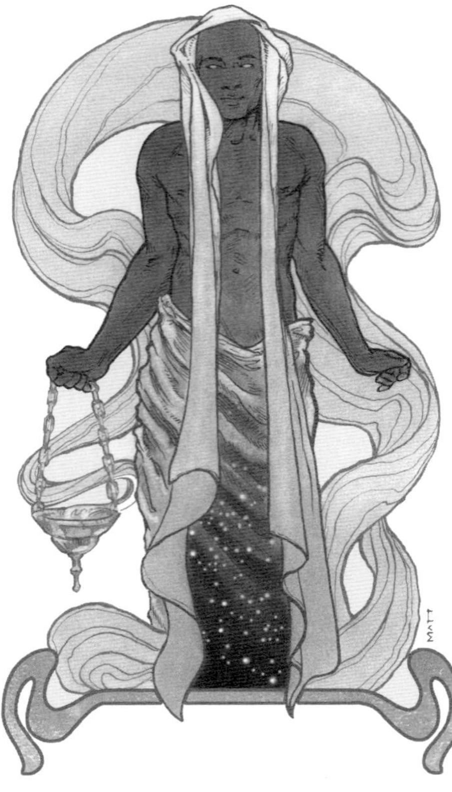

THE NIGHT

The Night transports deep, dark, dreamy scents with him. He moves slowly and effortlessly through the streets. His incense spills from the censer, coloring the air with its perfume. The smoke hangs thick in the air, blanketing the world in darkness. The Night wears the stars at his waist. Each speck twinkles with his movement, blinking in and out with each step. He wears a head wrap filled with the colors of the sky. The cover appears white at the top and then darkens into the daytime glow cast by the sun. He walks everywhere, bringing dreams and nightmares to everyone as the day falls away to meet the shadows.

Meanings: Don't be afraid of the dark; greet the shadows.

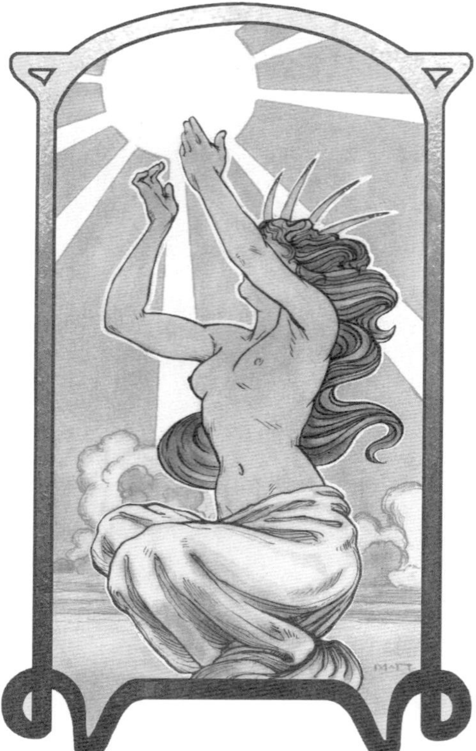

THE LIGHT

The goddess of the day holds her arms up to the light of the sun. She gives reverence to the life-sustaining rays, which bring heat and light. The sun sets the world ablaze, illuminating every part and every corner. Nothing escapes the fire. She brings happiness and illumination to the land. Wake up. It is time to get to work. Begin putting your desires into motion. You can achieve anything you set your heart to in this light. You might feel exposed by the brightness. It is alright. Let the anxiety pass; you have got this. Everything is as it should be. Give into the desires of the light and grow.

Meanings: Praise the day; know you are on the right path.

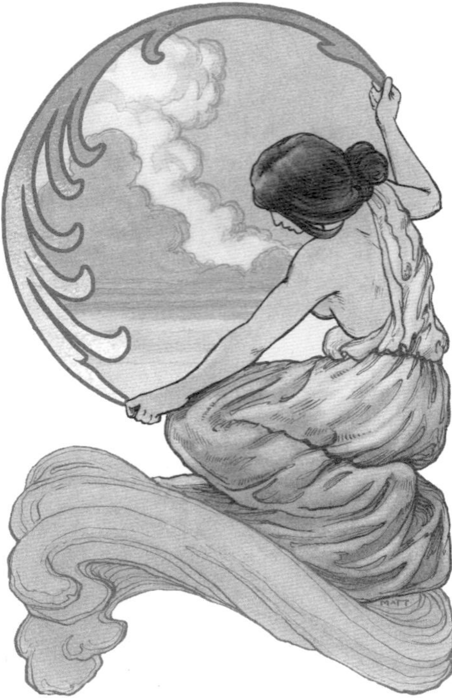
MATT

THE GATE

Portals appear at the corners of our eyes, which we can almost visualize if we squint. Some who see these portals know them for what they are. They have the gift of opening the small tear in the fabric of the world's material at will. The woman at the gate steps towards the rip and her fingers find the edges of the gate. She reaches out and traces the portal's edges and, gently, she tugs the sides apart. The space opens. The air's salty scent teases the corners of her lips as the soft sounds of ocean waves flow into our world. She continues pulling open the portal until there is a window big enough for someone to step through. She smiles out to the other side and walks away. The portal is open and now waits to welcome the traveler.

Meanings: Look deeper into the situation; what you want lies on the other side, just step through.

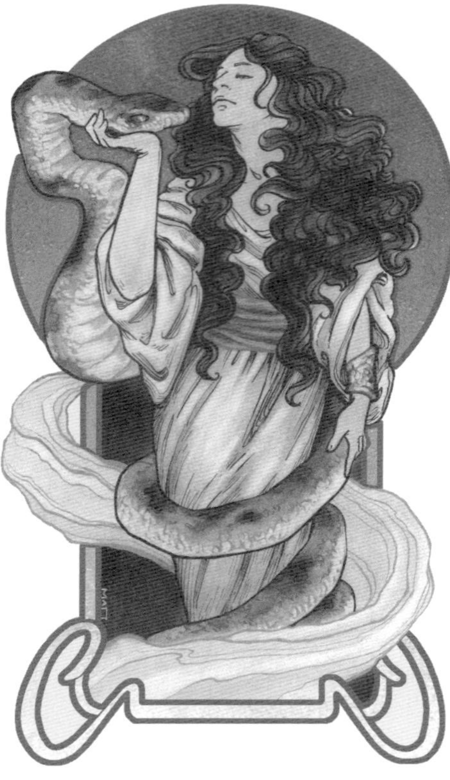

THE PROPHET

Humanity has always been drawn in by symbols. They stick with us, creating a language of their own. Beware of high tide; skip the thirteenth floor; toss salt over a shoulder. The Prophet knows the value of these signs. They appear subtle, whispering small curses and boons to those who listen. The Prophet knows where to look for these signs both in the external and internal worlds. She befriends the snake. She takes on an otherworldly air. She has a pearl of profound wisdom from which you can learn when you are ready to ask and receive.

Meanings: Follow the signs you are receiving; listen to the voices inside you.

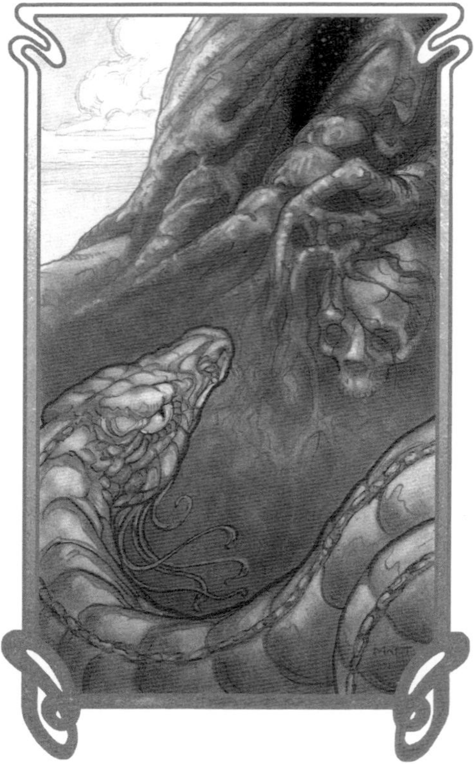

THE SERPENT

At the base of the world tree lives a serpent. He hungers and gnaws incessantly at the roots, seeking sustenance. He does not care that this tree serves a higher purpose nor that the worlds connected to the tree require it to remain stable. Without the tree, the worlds break apart and fade away. The serpent hungers and desires to consume everything and anything that stands in his way. He stays beneath the soil, devouring roots in his path, awaiting the time when he will be released from the tree to reunite with his brethren.

Meanings: Beware of dishonest people. Stay the course despite the stress.

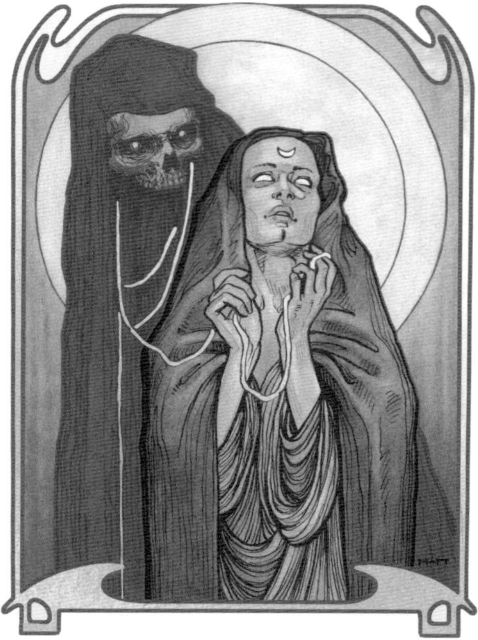

DEATH MOTHER

The delicate chains clatter and shimmer against the cloak. The sound is faint, a dying gasp from the soul. The Death Mother caresses the golden glitter between her fingertips. She knows everything about the departed. She knows how Death consumes their souls. The chains flow between the two of them, binding them over time. He gathers the newly deceased while she takes the measure of their worth. Eventually, she will assign them their final resting places. They work silently and steadily under cover of the moonlit skies, drawing spirits out and sending them onto the next stage of their journey.

Meanings: You are feeling tied down to something that no longer serves you; free yourself.

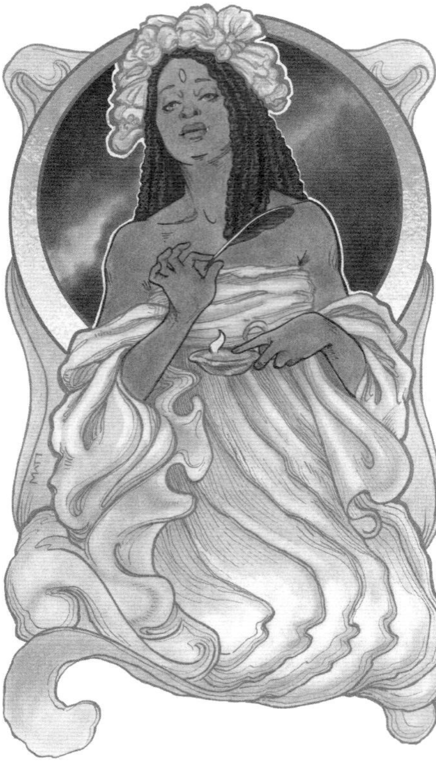

MEMORY

Memory is a delicate thing; it weighs as much as a feather and is just as fragile. Wave the feather one way, and the glimmer of the moment it captured appears as accurately as if it just happened. Dance the feather in a different direction and the memory fades, or changes, the details growing dim and dull. Flames rise from a golden bowl. They burn, distorting anything they touch, the heat warping the surface. Moments affected by the flame bend and buckle, turning into something less than they were. Details fade, the mind fearful of holding onto what was once true. Hold onto the truth by placing it into service to the future.

Meanings: Be mindful of the memories you desire to keep; let your memories drive your imagination to new heights.

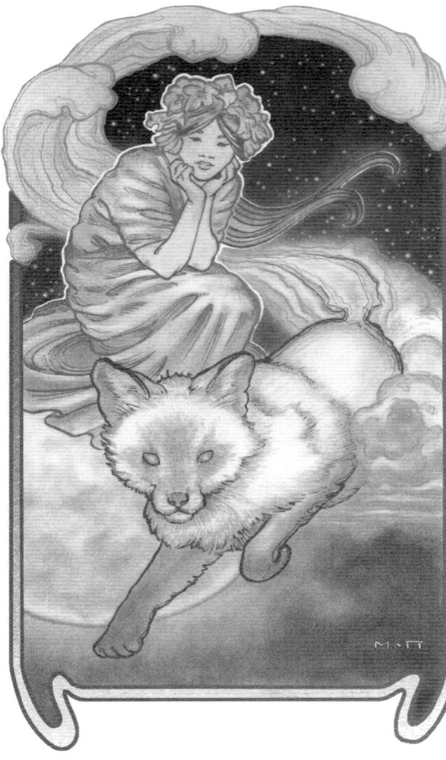

RABBIT AND FOX

Ever wonder why there's a rabbit on the moon? Of all the creatures on Earth, the rabbit was the most generous. One day Lady Luna visited Earth. All the animals gathered around to greet this new visitor and they brought her gifts. Some brought wood; others gathered fruit. The fox gathered fish from the river, while the poor rabbit offered grass. The rabbit told the Lady to make a fire from the grass and wood. In return, he offered his body so the lovely Lady would live. In return, she brought the rabbit back to life and took him to the moon to always live with her.

Meanings: Generosity begets gifts; always offer what you can.

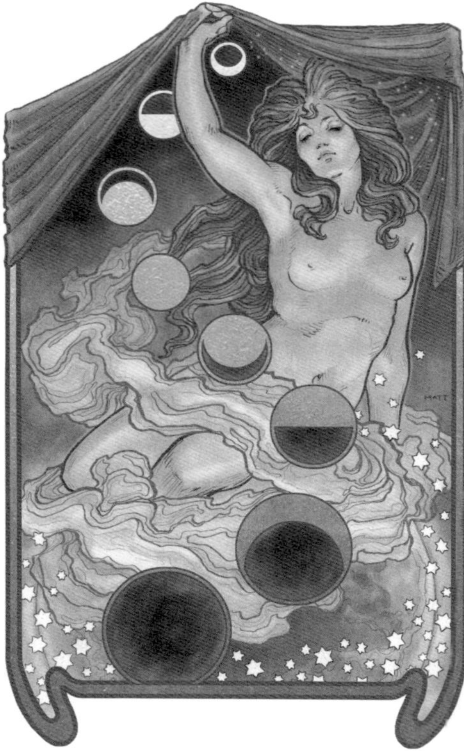
MATT

THE SHADOW

Gaia pulls the veil of the universe high into the heavens to reveal the line of moons spinning down the Milky Way from dark to full and back again. Her action turns around, giving us the time to delineate between the waking moments and the dreamlike states that murmur into our ears. The shadow phase of the moon provides us with the perspective to see clearly. Use this time to discern reality from imagination. When the planet is in its shadow phase, it is a powerfully magical time that allows us to see. It is an honor to gain access to the dreams of the universe. Use this time wisely.

Meanings: Follow your dreams; allow the childlike magic to flow into your life.

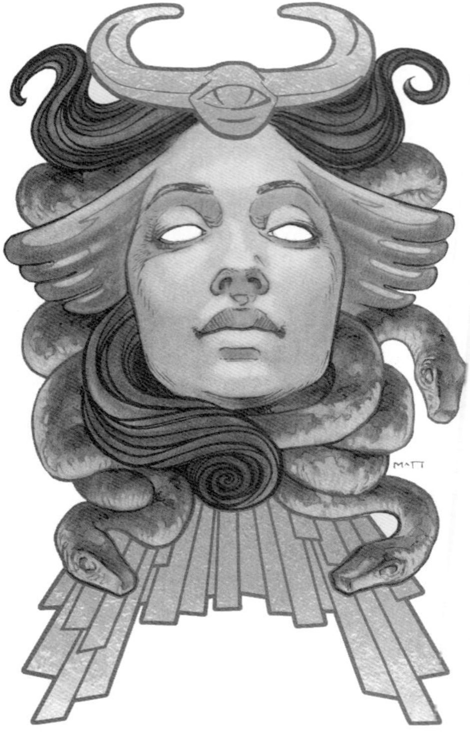
MATT

THE SEER

They know. They have the power to open their third eye and see past what is known and peer right into the unknown. The Seer honors the gifts the gods have bestowed upon them. They allow their imagination to tell them what will come and how to manage the flow of information. Snakes wrap around their neck, protecting, defending all the words and visions of the Seer. Going up to meet them invokes the will of the gods. Are you ready to hear what they have to tell you? Can you handle the news they will tell you about what is coming into your life, for better or worse?

Meanings: Listen to the universe in order to bring the dreams of insight. Locate the balance between fate and free will.

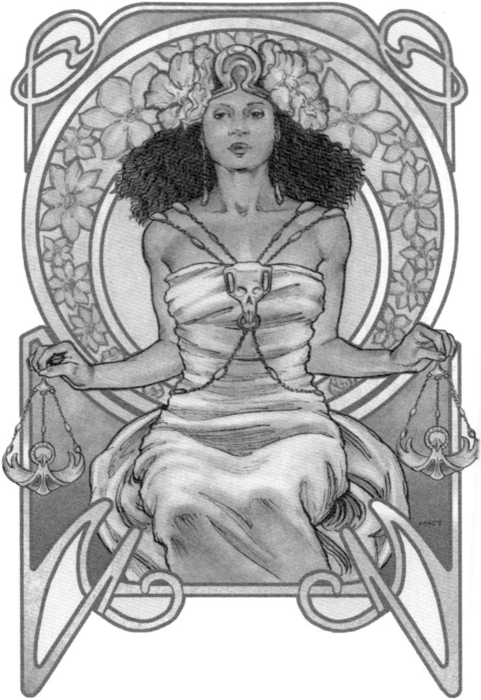

THE SCALES

She holds the scales of justice delicately between her fingers. She carefully weighs every spoken word people utter in her presence. Each nuance, each word choice petitioners make, gives their position away. Determining right from wrong requires an intricate skill. Not everyone can do what she can do. Flowers decorate her hair, showing the beauty that happens when the scales pass judgment. Her golden clothing matches the small scales dangling in each hand. If you look closely, one seems higher than the other. Did the results bring positive or negative outcomes? Only history will tell.

Meanings: Listen to what is going on in the situation and make a decision to benefit your world; bring proper judgment back to the world.

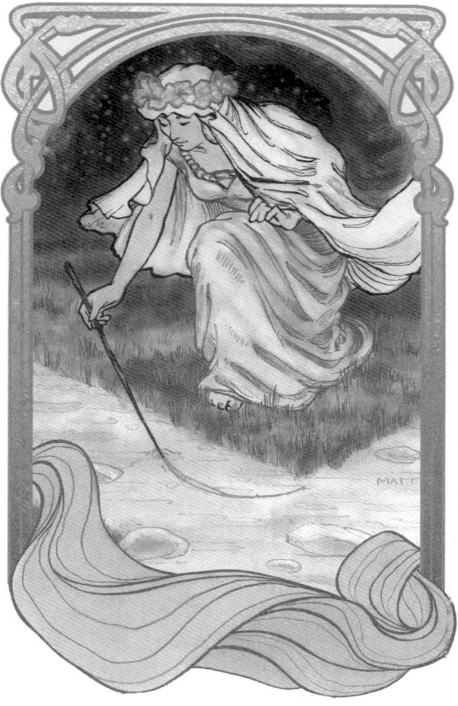
MATT

THE PATH

Paths are birthed by treading across the same area of land over days, months, or years. Sometimes the way is made by a single individual; sometimes large groups of creatures dig grooves out of the landscape. Your spiritual path is unique to your journey. It has many curves, peaks and valleys. It takes repetition to create a well-worn track. When we look back from where we came from, we see how the pattern got made. If the Path card visited you today, you might want to look at where you are going. Is it where you still want to go? Make any corrections in the course now.

Meanings: Keep moving forward; make any adjustments based on your desires.

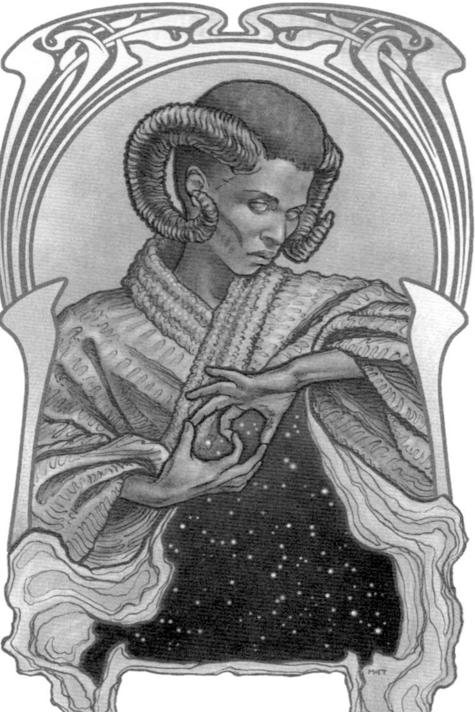

BALANCE

The idea of a binary is a human concept. We contain both one and another inside our genetic makeup. Balance sits outside of this duality. They follow their vibration, their own story. They can often be positive, revealing the good that sits inside us all. They can also be gloomy as they give in to the dark emotions that lie feral, waiting to attack. Balance sits somewhere in between. They know what it is like to carry both sides. Balance blends the best and the worst presenting us all a new opportunity to experience the whole of creation.

Meanings: Look for the positive in the negative; temper your emotions.

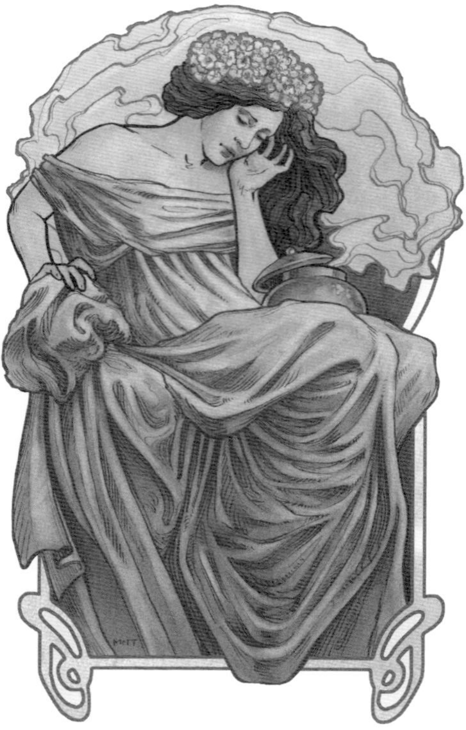

THE GIFT

Smoke rising up behind her, Pandora sits in her chair, pondering what the jar contained. Was it a good idea to release the potent magic contained in such a small vessel? She does not know what will become of her gift just yet. Only time can tell what will happen to the world as the gift spreads out from the tarnished jar. Pandora wears a simple lavender robe showing her devotion to Zeus. It also shows the gift of wisdom and generosity attributed to her.

Meanings: Be careful of stepping into situations you may not be able to get out of; retreat from complicated situations.

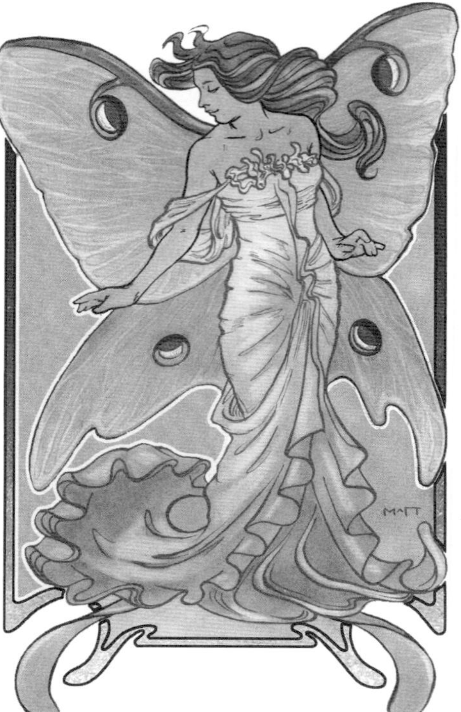
MATT

LUNA MOTH

A luna moth lives for only a short time. Within that period, they mate, eat, and then die, only to have their offspring carry on their legacy. Their unique coloring attracts much interest. Their wings appear to glow, and they have circles that look like moons on them. Some cultures associate the luna moth with a symbol of transformation and change. Other cultures suggest the luna moth represents a person's soul as it leaves a dead body. No matter where you place the luna moth's spiritual virtue, it is a stunning specimen of Lepidoptera.

Meanings: It's time to transform bad habits into good ones; take a healthy break from your obsessions to gain revelations.

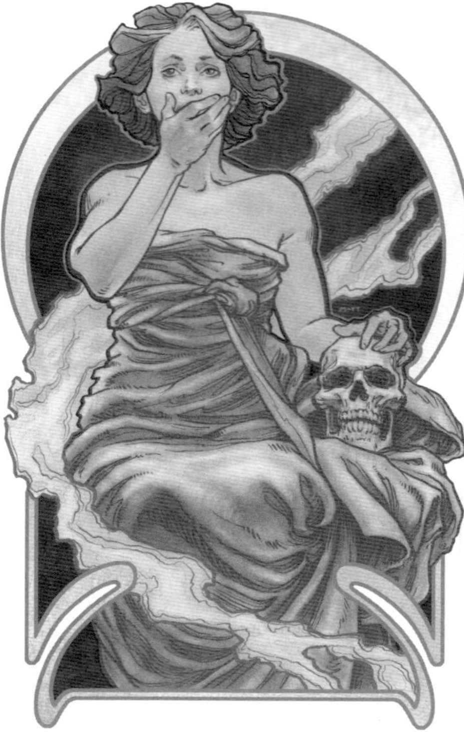

THE SILENCE

No amount of clarity or visualization is possible without distancing oneself from the noise of the world. Turning inward helps us become more in tune with the significant presence that fills the universe. It allows us to lay ourselves bare to it and to connect with and ponder the greater meaning of life. It can be challenging to take ourselves out of the flood of distractions we deal with minute by minute. But our ancestors stand by our side, waiting to silently guide us along our path. Their experience and guidance are indispensable in our journey. The Silence rests her arm against a skull. Some cultures view skulls as an ultimate symbol of a life well lived. It represents our awareness of their message that echos to us from the other side of the veil. Our legacy is our real teacher to the world.

Meanings: Seek out a place of stillness to hear what you need; take time to meditate.

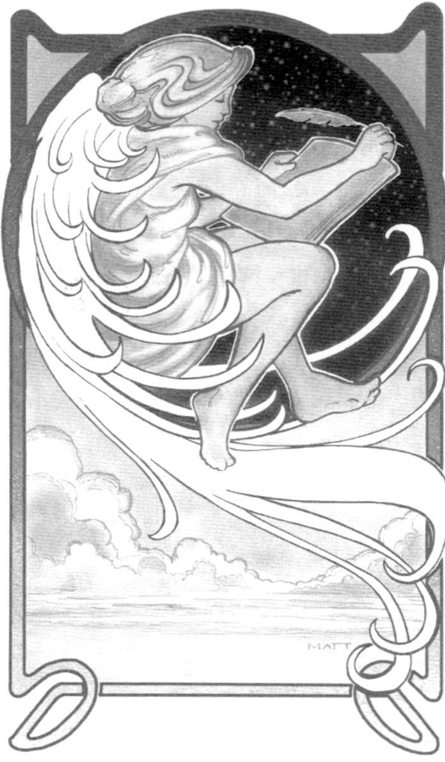
MATT

THE WORD

Stories and storytelling have been with us since the beginning. Our minds are designed to share our experiences with each other. We crave the sharing of stories to remind us that we are connected through our words. The Word leans into her wings. She steadies a stack of parchment on her lap, her knees curled up to meet the paper. The girl holds a plume in her right hand, poised to strike the page at any moment. Her eyes remain closed, engrossed in the visions of the story her mind describes. When she is ready, a new story will get inked on the page.

Meanings: Write your story down; have a playful attitude towards life.

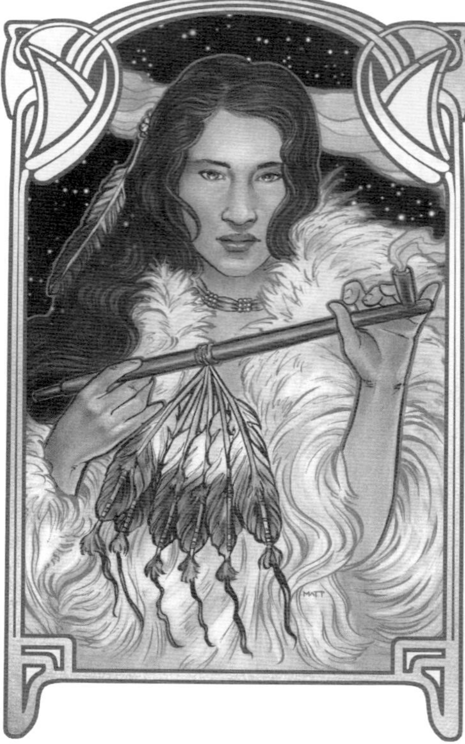
MATT

WHITE BUFFALO

White Buffalo brought the sacred traditions to the Indigenous American peoples. She stepped from the clouds to help the Lakota people survive. The White Buffalo holds out a sacred pipe filled with tobacco as a peace offering. The six feathers that hang off the shaft represent one of the six rites she showed her people. The seventh rite hangs off from her black hair. She wears the pelt of a white buffalo, the honored beast that gifted her name. The arrival of the White Buffalo is a sign of restoring harmony and spirituality to a troubled world. Follow traditions that bring nature back into balance. Do your part to make a change in our environment.

Meanings: It's time to restore harmony to the world. Be mindful of spirituality in your life.

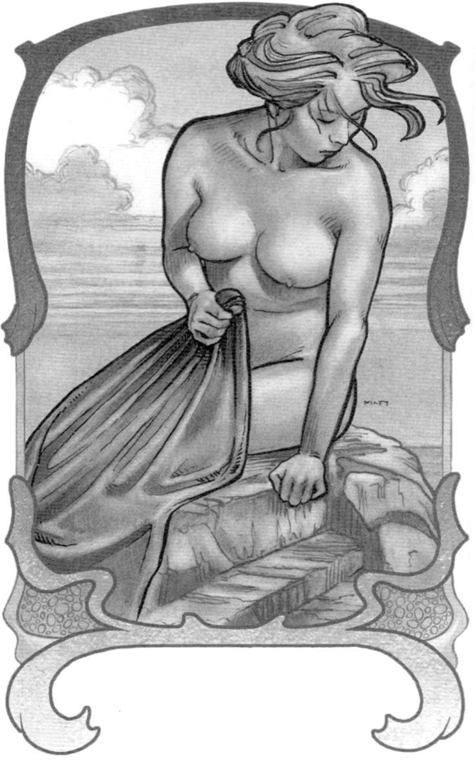

THE SELKIE

In Scottish mythology, selkies are shape-shifting creatures who can change from seals to humans by shedding their skin. Myths say that if a man finds a female selkie's discarded skin, they can marry the selkie while she's in her human body. The man hides the skin, trapping her against her true nature, never allowing her to return to the sea and her kin. The only way for a selkie to receive her freedom is to find and take back her skin. Male selkies are unusually handsome and lure women to them. They are also where we get the myth of the merfolk.

Meanings: Feeling like your freedom is compromised, there is a loss of self-control.

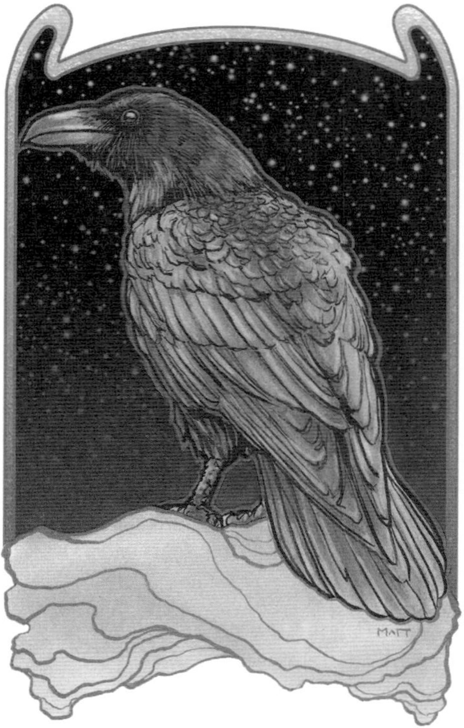
MATT

RAVEN

Humans underestimate ravens. They are cunning and intelligent creatures who use tools to get to what they want. It's no wonder most mythology refers to them as psychopomps. A psychopomp is a guide who leads the deceased to their resting place. Ravens have been heralds of the dying for as long as civilization can recall. If Raven has come to you today, it's time to get crafty. Use your intelligence to make a vital shift happen. Honor those who live in memory. Set up an altar and pay respect to the dead.

Meanings: It's time to get crafty with the situation. Honor your ancestors.

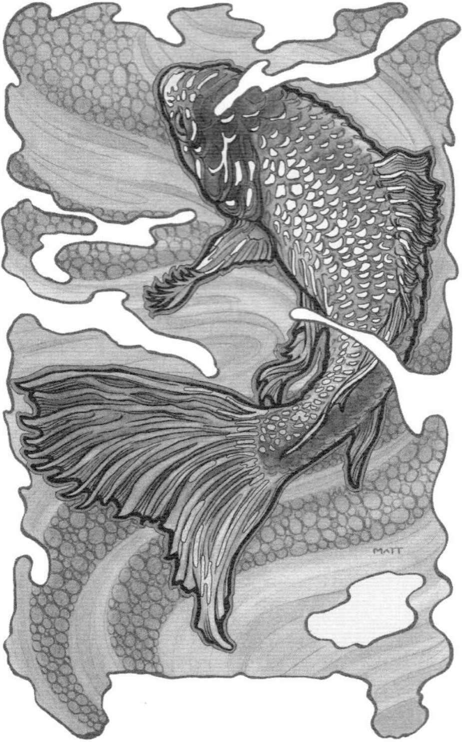
MATT

KOI FISH

In Japanese myth, the koi fish swims upstream along the Yellow River. Once it conquers its many challenges and reaches the river's head, it transforms into a majestic dragon. The Japanese view the koi fish as a symbol of aspiration and good fortune, which is manifest through determination and hard work. You have the power to transform your life.

Meanings: You are ready to transform; good prosperity and wealth are on their way.

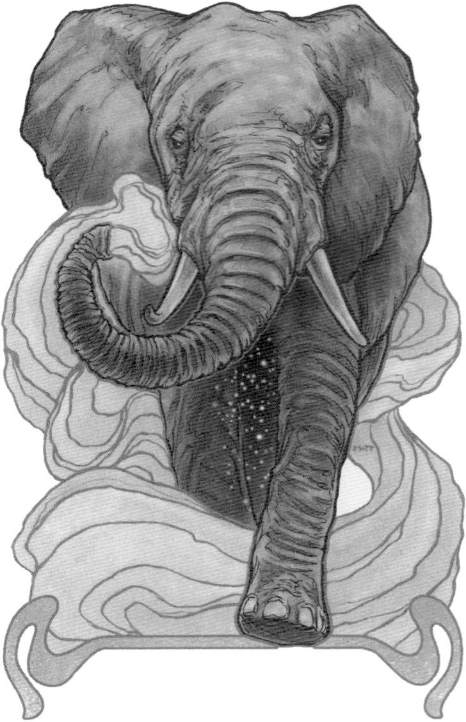

ELEPHANT

An elephant never forgets. Or so the saying goes. However, these giant gentle beasts are much more than that. They are highly social animals that form family bonds for life. They are extremely loyal and stick together. If the Elephant card has graced your home today, consider yourself fortunate and lucky indeed. Take time to think about what strengths you have and who is in your social circle. Reach out to those who you have not connected with, or tackle a new creative hobby.

Meanings: Take time to engage with others. Look toward others who can be loyal to you.

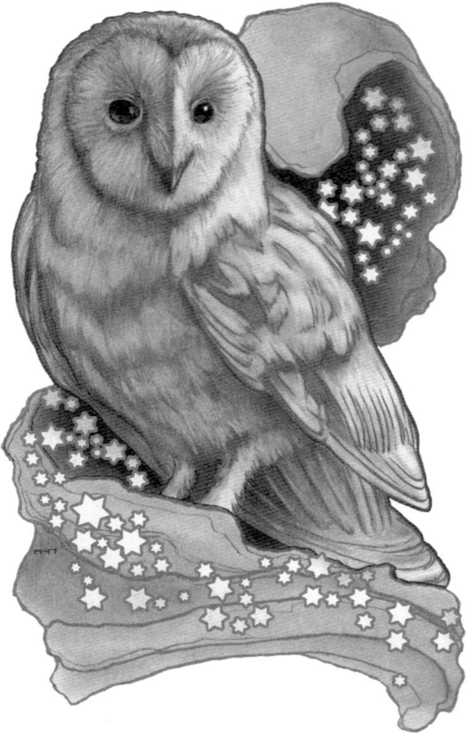

WHITE OWL

The white owl has been a recurring symbol spanning thousands of years. Their white color is often associated with purity and youthfulness. The White Owl embodies all species of owls' traits in readings: knowledge, wisdom, and exceptional insight. They have extraordinary long-range vision for hunting prey. This ability to see through distance and time gives the reader a clear insight into what actions are needed when a message is delivered. In the *Dreamscape Oracle*, owls are messengers who carry critical communications in and out of the portals.

Meanings: Time to undertake a new spiritual pursuit. Ponder the cycle of life and death.

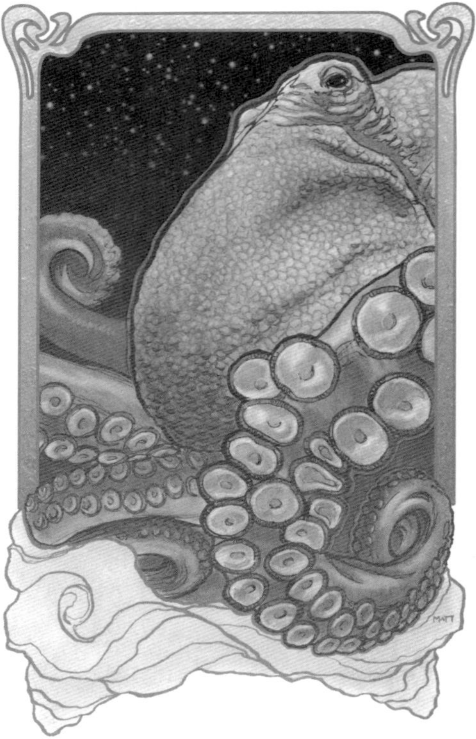
MATT

OCTOPUS

The octopus is a highly intelligent invertebrate whose skin contains chromatophores, which allows the octopus to adapt to any situation. They are a symbol of multitasking due to the actions all their limbs can handle at once. If the Octopus has come into your life, it may be time for you to juggle all the tasks you have going on right now. Make a list, set some priorities, and get at it. The ability to camouflage themselves allows them to slip under the radar and wait for their desires. You can call upon the octopus energy to help you wait until the right moment to get what you want.

Meanings: Time to prioritize and get things done; patience and intellect lead you to success.

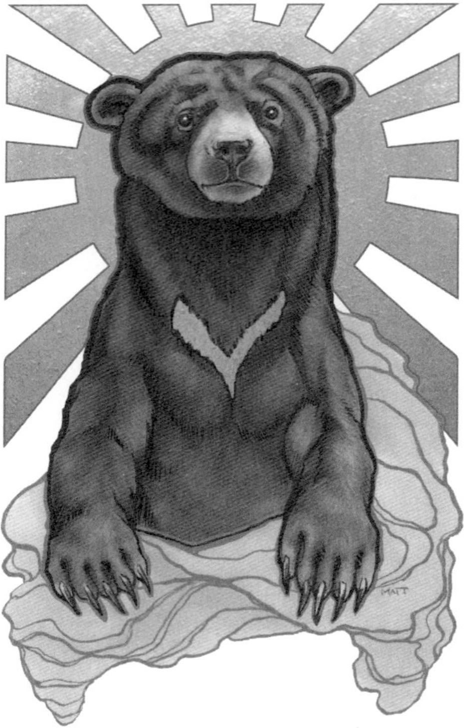
MATT

SUN BEAR

Sun bears live predominately in Southeast Asia, where they prefer to spend most of their time watching from the trees. The distinctive golden chest patch reflects the warmth and life of our sun. The sun bear is considered the embodiment of spiritual power and strength. Their intuition and self-reflection help one to heal through harmony and balance. As part of the *Ursidae* family, they also share common spiritual traits of intuition and introspection. The strength of bear medicine is seated with the power to restore harmony and balance—to heal. Many cultures refer to the bear spirit as the Great Healer.

Meanings: Summon the strength to help steady your spirit. Listen to your intuition and let it guide you.

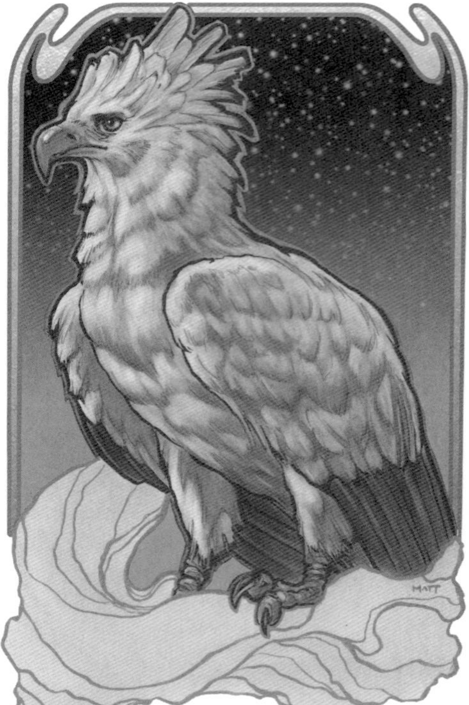
MATT

HARPY EAGLE

The Harpy Eagle in the *Dreamscape Oracle* is a female from the American variety. Harpy eagles are a sign that you need to change something in your life. They represent your strength and none of your weaknesses. The Harpy Eagle comes to you via visions in your sleep time and your waking days. When it appears, heed the message and take a good look at what is out of balance in your life. Take stock of your life. Are you where you want to be emotionally, physically, and financially? Now is the time to envision where you want to be and who you want in your life. Harness harpy eagle power when times are tough, and you need some extra help to guide you to the other side.

Meanings: Time to reassess your life and adjust accordingly; listen to the messages spirit is sending you.

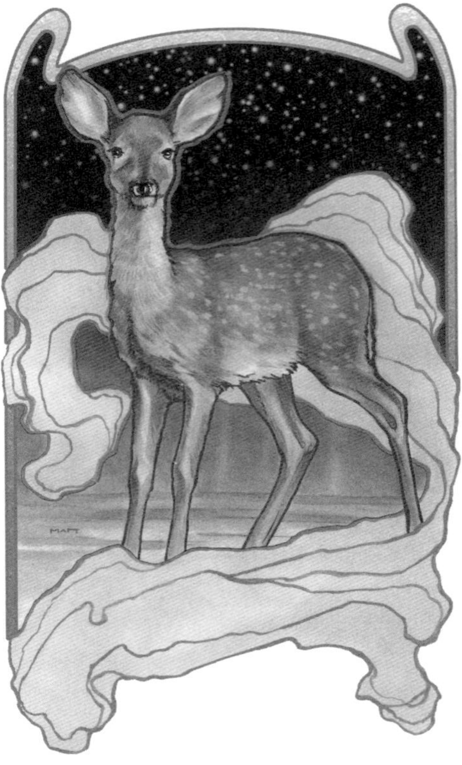

FAWN

Fawn is the term given to young deer in their first year. They are lighter colored, which helps them blend into their surroundings to survive. In many cultures, fawns symbolize new financial beginnings. They can also indicate when a significant life change is heading in your direction. Use fawn energy when you want to change your life outcomes. It is a good omen when fawn comes to visit you in this deck. Get ready for change to make its appearance, both good or bad. You may also want to look at your bank statements. How can you improve your monetary status at this time?

Meanings: Significant change is coming your way; a new financial opportunity may appear.

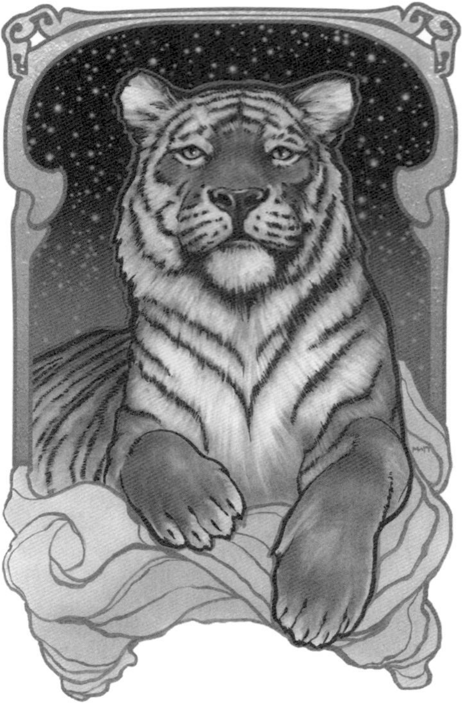

TIGER

Tigers are some of the most recognizable cats in the world. They are territorial and mostly solitary, but are social creatures when they go hunting. Diverse cultures fear their ferocity and view tigers as a formidable force. Many people call upon tiger energy to overcome obstacles and reclaim personal power. With their dwindling habitat, tigers have had to adapt to the constant changes humanity imposes upon them. Call upon Tiger when you are dealing with adverse situations that need your assistance. Show your strength and don't back down until you know when things are in your favor.

Meanings: Overcome adversity through personal power. Exert a strong will to push through tough times.

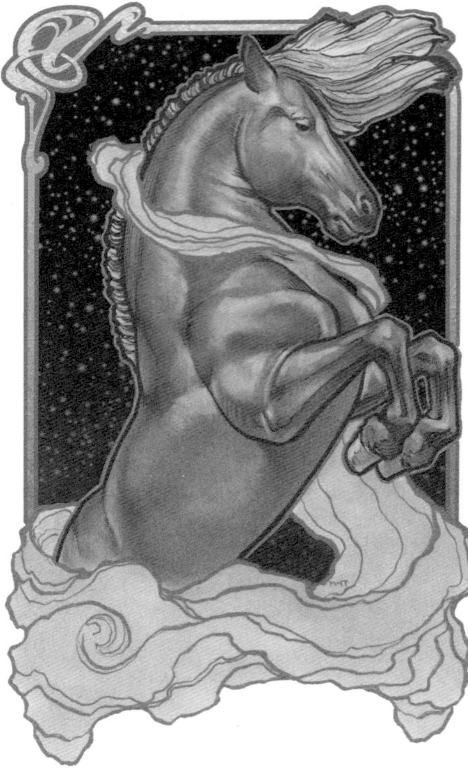

PALOMINO

Horses are among the longest surviving companions to humanity throughout the ages. They are reliable, loyal and hard-working creatures often associated with power, speed and strength. A palomino refers to a breed of golden horses found in the American West. The majestic white mane and vibrant chestnut coats of the palomino make them stand out from other horses. They are well known for their unbridled wildness and strength of will. When palomino comes into your world, it's time to pay attention to your needs, step up to do the work, and get those projects done. Conversely, allow yourself to step out of the stables on occasion. The Palomino also reminds us to run wild and be free to soak in the warm summer sun while we can.

Meanings: Allow yourself to roam free on occasion. It's time to put in the hard work to meet your goals.

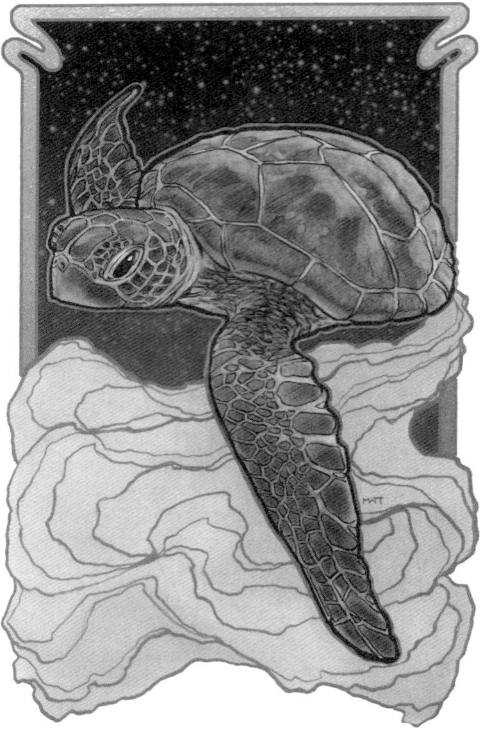
MATT

SEA TURTLE

The sea turtle is a gentle creature with a long life span and can swim over vast distances. It can take decades to reach full maturity, granting them insight and wisdom only accumulated through time and experience. Sea turtles represent the journey and share their infinite patience as you walk the path and learn from the lessons given along the way. When the Sea Turtle comes into your life, it may be time to look at the big picture and determine your needs for the long haul. Are you ready for the future? Now is the time to start planning.

Meanings: Enjoy the journey of your life; start planning for the future.

THE DREAMSCAPE ORACLE SPREAD

The *Dreamscape Oracle* evokes imagery of stepping out from what you already know and into the hero's journey where you wander around, meeting new characters and taking on new challenges. Use this spread to seek out a new goal or desire. Let the first step propel you to success on the journey you're commencing.

| 1 | 2 | 3 |

Card One: The Seeker

What do I seek? This card provides information about what you desire. How close to manifestation is this desire?

Card Two: The First Step

What direction do I take on my first step? It's hard to step out when you do not know where to go. The advice from this card gives you focus and information on how to act. It's a verb, the first action to take in getting what you desire. Take this first step forward, and you'll find that the rest of the steps fall in place, naturally giving you a lovely stepping stone path to completion. If you find you need more advice or actions, you can add more cards until you receive the desired conclusion.

Card Three: The Outcome

What will happen if I attain this goal? While some goals and dreams take many more steps, it's always nice to see if you are on the right track after choosing a direction. This card reveals the temperature of your goal. Receiving a positive card helps you to stay on the right track. Getting a negative card might mean you need to think about changing course, or adding more steps to take.

PERFORMING YOUR FIRST READING

Many new readers get nervous about drawing oracle cards. They worry about if they're shuffling correctly or if they're reading the card right. There's no right or wrong way to interpret a card. You will develop personal styles and rituals around using the *Dreamscape Oracle* deck. When you are ready to begin your relationship with the cards, follow this simple process:

Think about what is going on in your life. What dreams and desires do you want? Are there any questions you want answers to? Think about what you want to ask the deck. Crafting a question does help you receive precise answers. "How can I modify my attitude at work to get better results?" and "What can I do to release this emotional feeling?" can yield better answers than "Will they marry me?" or "Will I get more money soon?"

Now that you have your question handy, it's time to shuffle the cards. There's no rule in how you mix your cards. Just make sure they're well blended.

Draw a card and then think about what it is saying to you. You can also lay the cards down in a pattern known as a spread. You could try out the three-card spread in the previous section or find many others online or in other divination books.

Use the meanings in this booklet to interpret your reading. It's okay if you get a different result than the one described in these pages. Go with your gut. Sometimes what you think a card means is more accurate to the situation.

Write down your thoughts, any meanings, and draft an answer to your question. It may take time to create a clear, coherent message. Learning the art of divination takes time. Don't feel frustrated if you don't understand what the cards are saying at first.

ABOUT THE ARTIST

Matt Hughes is a self-taught traditional artist focusing on the aesthetic approaches referred to today as "The Golden Age of Illustration." His style combines inspiration from the Art Nouveau movement, the Pre-Raphaelite movement, and the Symbolist movement to produce an artistic expression all his own. He is the creator of *Ethereal Visions: Illuminated Tarot Deck* and contributed to *Pride Tarot: A Collaborative Deck*.

www.EtherealVisionsPub.com

WOODSTOCK, GEORGIA

NOTES

NOTES

For our complete line of tarot decks, books, meditation cards, oracle sets, and other inspirational products please visit our website:

www.usgamesinc.com

Follow us on f t p o

U.S. GAMES SYSTEMS, INC.
179 Ludlow Street
Stamford, CT 06902 USA
203-353-8400
Order Desk 800-544-2637
FAX 203-353-8431